I Help Out on the Farm

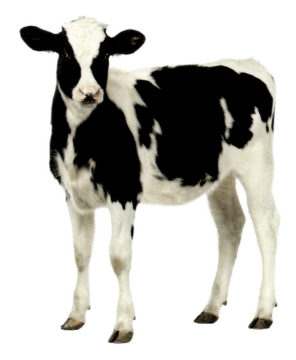

AMY CULLIFORD

A Crabtree Roots Book

Crabtree Publishing
crabtreebooks.com

School-to-Home Support for Caregivers and Teachers

This book helps children grow by letting them practice reading. Here are a few guiding questions to help the reader with building his or her comprehension skills. Possible answers appear here in red.

Before Reading:
- What do I think this book is about?
    - *I think this book is about helping with outside jobs.*
    - *I think this book is about helping with farm animals.*
- What do I want to learn about this topic?
    - *I want to learn more about jobs I can do outside to help out.*
    - *I want to learn how to plant crops.*

During Reading:
- I wonder why...
    - *I wonder why crops need to be watered.*
    - *I wonder what cows like to eat.*
- What have I learned so far?
    - *I have learned that it's fun to do outside jobs.*
    - *I have learned that shovels are used to dig up the ground.*

After Reading:
- What details did I learn about this topic?
    - *I have learned that planting is part of helping out on the farm.*
    - *I have learned that it looks fun to help out with animals.*
- Read the book again and look for the vocabulary words.
    - *I see the word **farm** on page 3 and the word **crops** on page 8. The other vocabulary words are found on page 14.*

I want to help out on the **farm**.

I help dig up the **ground**.

I help **plant**.

I help water the **crops**.

I help with
the **animals**.

I like to help out on the farm!

Word List
Sight Words

dig	on	up
help	out	want
I	the	water
like	to	with

Words to Know

animals **crops** **farm**

ground **plant**

35 Words

I want to help out on the **farm**.

I help dig up the **ground**.

I help **plant**.

I help water the **crops**.

I help with the **animals**.

I like to help out on the farm!

I Help Out on the Farm

Written by: Amy Culliford
Designed by: Rhea Wallace
Series Development: James Earley
Proofreader: Melissa Boyce
Educational Consultant: Marie Lemke M.Ed.

Photographs:
Shutterstock: Attasit Saentep: cover; Eric Isseelee: p. 1; Natalia Belay: p.3; Sergiy Bykhunenko: p. 5; Max Kegfire: p. 7; Torychemistry: p. 8-9; Zurijeta: p. 13

Crabtree Publishing

crabtreebooks.com   800-387-7650
Copyright © 2025 Crabtree Publishing
All rights reserved. No part of this publication may be reproduced, stored in a retrieval system or be transmitted in any form or by any means, electronic, mechanical, photocopying, recording, or otherwise, without the prior written permission of Crabtree Publishing. In Canada: We acknowledge the financial support of the Government of Canada through the Canada Book Fund for our publishing activities.

Printed in the USA
062024/CG20240201

Published in Canada
Crabtree Publishing
616 Welland Ave.
St. Catharines, Ontario
L2M 5V6

Published in the United States
Crabtree Publishing
347 Fifth Ave
Suite 1402-145
New York, NY 10016

Library and Archives Canada Cataloguing in Publication
Available at Library and Archives Canada

Library of Congress Cataloging-in-Publication Data
Available at the Library of Congress

Hardcover: 978-1-0398-3833-8
Paperback: 978-1-0398-3918-2
Ebook (pdf): 978-1-0398-4002-7
Epub: 978-1-0398-4074-4